LIVING IN THE WILD: PRIMATES

GORILLAS

Lori McManus

Heinemann
LIBRARY

Chicago, Illinois

www.capstonepub.com
Visit our website to find out more information about Heinemann-Raintree books.

To order:
☎ Phone 888-454-2279
💻 Visit www.capstonepub.com
to browse our catalog and order online.

Edited by Abby Colich, Jilly Hunt, and Vaarunika Dharmapala
Designed by Victoria Allen
Picture research by Tracy Cummins
Original illustrations © Capstone Global Library Ltd 2012
Illustrations by Oxford Designers & Illustrators and HL Studios

Originated by Capstone Global Library Ltd
Printed and bound in the United States of America, North Mankato, MN

15 14 13 12
10 9 8 7 6 5 4 3 2

Library of Congress Cataloging-in-Publication Data
McManus, Lori.
 Gorillas / Lori McManus.—1st ed.
  p. cm.—(Living in the wild: primates)
 Includes bibliographical references and index.
 ISBN 978-1-4329-5863-3 (hb)—ISBN 978-1-4329-5870-1 (pb) 1. Gorilla—Juvenile literature. I. Title.
 QL737.P96M45 2012
 599.884—dc22   2011012894

052012
006696

Acknowledgments
We would like to thank the following for permission to reproduce photographs: Alamy p. 41 (© Orokiet); Corbis pp. 15 (© Yann Arthus-Bertrand), 35 (© Bettmann); FLPA pp. 8 (Terry Whittaker), 17 (Ariadne Van Zandbergen), 26 (Terry Whittaker), 27 (Konrad Wothe/Minden Pictures), 34 (Konrad Wothe); Getty Images pp. 25 (Buena Vista Images), 28 (Andy Rouse); istockphoto pp. 7 (© Elliot Hurwitt), 20 (© DaveThomasNZ), 44 (© Elliot Hurwitt); National Geographic Stock pp. 6 (Joel Sartore), 13 (Michael Nichols), 23 (Suzi Eszterhas/Minden Pictures), 24 (Peter G. Veit), 29 (Ian Nichols), 36 (Gerry Ellis/Minden Pictures), 39 (Michael Nichols); Newscom p. 33 (CB2/ZOB/WENN.com); Photolibrary pp. 4 (Berndt Fischer), 37 (Michel Gunther); Photoshot p. 19 (Andy Rouse/NHPA); Shutterstock pp. 9 (© Alan Jeffery) 11 (© Ronald van der Beek), 24 (© Steffen Foerster Photography), 22 (© Eric Gevaert), 31 (© Peter J. Kovacs), 32 (© neelsky), 43 (© Eric Gevaert).

Cover photograph of a mountain gorilla in Rwanda, reproduced with permission of Photolibrary (J-L. Klein & M-L. Hubert).

Every effort has been made to contact copyright holders of any material reproduced in this book. Any omissions will be rectified in subsequent printings if notice is given to the publisher.

Disclaimer
All the Internet addresses (URLs) given in this book were valid at the time of going to press. However, due to the dynamic nature of the Internet, some addresses may have changed, or sites may have changed or ceased to exist since publication. While the author and publisher regret any inconvenience this may cause readers, no responsibility for any such changes can be accepted by either the author or the publisher.

Contents

What Are Primates? 4

What Are Gorillas? 6

How Are Gorillas Classified? 10

Where Do Gorillas Live? 12

What Adaptations Help Gorillas Survive? 16

What Do Gorillas Eat? 20

What Is a Gorilla's Life Cycle? 22

How Do Gorillas Behave? 26

How Intelligent Are Gorillas? 32

What Threats Do Gorillas Face? 36

How Can People Help Gorillas? 40

What Does the Future Hold for Gorillas? 42

Gorilla Profile 44

Glossary 46

Find Out More 47

Index 48

Some words are shown in bold, **like this**. You can find out what they mean by looking in the glossary.

What Are Primates?

Out of the bushes roll a group of youngsters playing follow the leader. Several adults relax nearby. Is this a playground in a park? No, it is a forest in Africa, where young gorillas play while their mothers watch.

Six key characteristics

Gorillas belong to a special group of animals called primates. Monkeys, lemurs, orangutans, and humans belong to this group. Primates are **mammals** that share six key characteristics:

1. Forward-facing eyes: Both eyes point in the same direction and can focus on the same object.

2. Eye sockets: The eyeball sits inside a hollow space protected by bone.

3. Grasping hands: The thumb can be used to grip or press against the other four fingers.

Like all primates, orangutans have hands that allow them to grip branches.

4. Nails: Most primates have fingers and toes ending in a flat nail that protects the tip.

5. Fingerprints: The skin on the fingertips and underside of the hand is bare and covered in a pattern of tiny ridges. Each primate's fingerprints are unique.

6. Large brains relative to their body size: Compared to many mammals, primates have large brains, which give them higher intelligence.

All primates, except for humans, are currently **endangered**. These special animals may soon disappear completely if they are not protected.

This map shows where in the world non-human primates live.

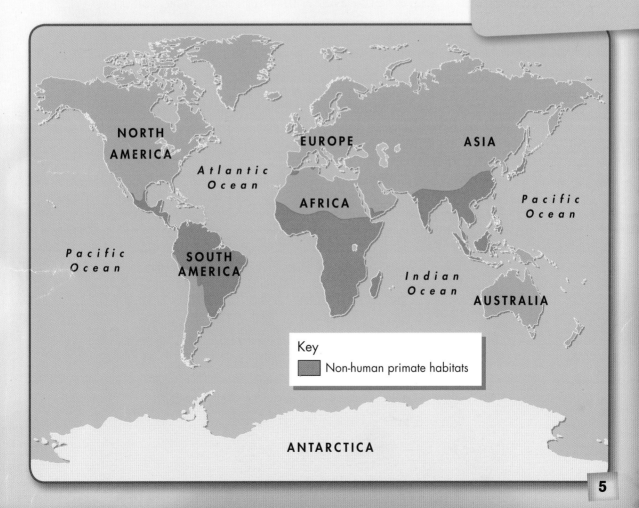

Key

Non-human primate habitats

What Are Gorillas?

Gorillas are the largest and heaviest primate. They are part of a group called apes, which also includes chimpanzees, orangutans, bonobos, gibbons, and humans. All apes have a large body size and weight. They have broad chests and long arms. Apes have big brains, and they do not have tails. Gorillas share similarities with other apes, yet their specific size, shape, and color set them apart.

Like all apes, this gorilla does not have a tail outside its body.

Size and shape

Gorillas are the largest apes on Earth. Males are always bigger than females. When standing upright, gorillas are about 5 inches (13 centimeters) shorter than average human adults. Although some male gorillas grow as heavy as 550 pounds (250 kilograms), most males weigh between 300 and 440 pounds (135 and 200 kilograms). Females weigh between about 150 and 200 pounds (70 and 90 kilograms).

A gorilla's shape is unusual among non-human apes. Its stomach is larger than its chest! This huge belly is due to the size of a gorilla's intestines, the stretchy tube attached to the stomach that absorbs **nutrients** from food. A gorilla's small intestine would be nearly 33 feet (10 meters) long if it were stretched out straight!

Gorillas' arms are much longer than their legs. They also have bigger muscles in their arms. Gorillas use their powerful arms for walking and finding food. They almost always walk on their hands and feet, even though they can stand up on their legs.

A gorilla's belly is even larger than its wide, powerful chest.

Hair and skin

Gorillas have dark black to brown-gray hair. This hair can be long and silky or short and thin, depending on where the gorillas live. As male gorillas age, the hair on their backs and upper thighs turns silvery-gray. Because of this change in color, adult males are sometimes called "silverbacks."

Under a gorilla's dark hair, the skin is also dark. Sometimes baby gorillas are born with patches of lighter skin that turn dark with age. Gorillas have skin without hair on the soles of their feet, palms of their hands, fingers, nose, lips, ears, and chest.

Gorillas have especially tough skin on their fingers. They use their knuckles for walking, and the thick skin protects them from injury. Gorillas, chimpanzees, and bonobos are the only animals to get around by "knuckle-walking."

Gorillas can move very fast when they knuckle-walk.

A big head

Gorillas have large heads. The back part of the head is higher than the front. This bony area, called the sagittal crest, supports the strong muscles needed to chew raw plants. A gorilla's large forehead protects its small eyes.

Another obvious feature on a gorilla's face is its wide, flat nose. Its nostrils are large. Although gorillas have a good sense of smell, they rely more on their eyesight than their sense of smell.

NOSEPRINTS

Scientists can tell gorillas apart by looking at their noses. Each gorilla's nose is unique, like a fingerprint.

Here you can see a gorilla's wide, flat nose, its large forehead, and the sagittal crest on the back of the head.

How Are Gorillas Classified?

Scientists **classify** gorillas into two main groups based on their similarities.

Classification of living things

All animals share basic characteristics. For example, they all eat food to get energy. However, some animals are more closely related than others.

Scientists usually divide living things into seven levels of classification: kingdom, phylum, class, order, family, genus, and **species**. These can be divided even further—for example, into suborder and family.

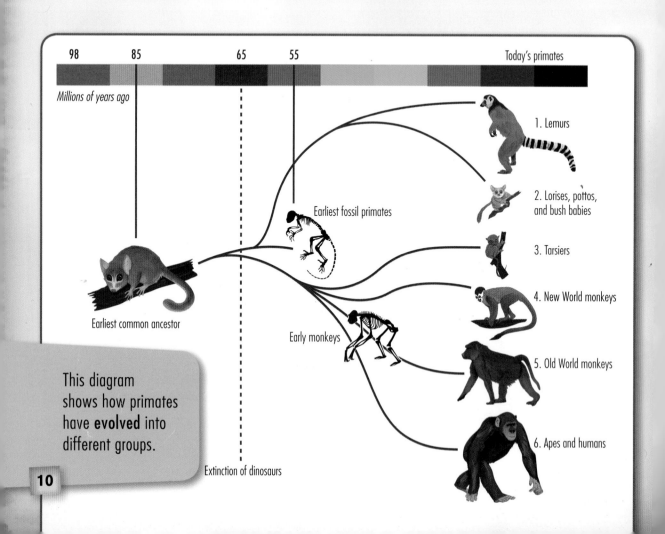

98   85   65   55   Today's primates

Millions of years ago

Earliest fossil primates

Earliest common ancestor

Early monkeys

Extinction of dinosaurs

1. Lemurs

2. Lorises, pottos, and bush babies

3. Tarsiers

4. New World monkeys

5. Old World monkeys

6. Apes and humans

This diagram shows how primates have **evolved** into different groups.

Classification of gorillas

Scientists once believed that all gorillas were similar enough to be classified as one species. However, gorillas in western Africa are smaller and have shorter hair than other gorillas. Eastern gorillas grow larger and have darker hair. In 2001 scientists classified gorillas into two species: the western gorilla and the eastern gorilla. These two species can be divided into even smaller groups, called subspecies— western lowland gorilla, (western) Cross River gorilla, eastern lowland gorilla, and (eastern) mountain gorilla.

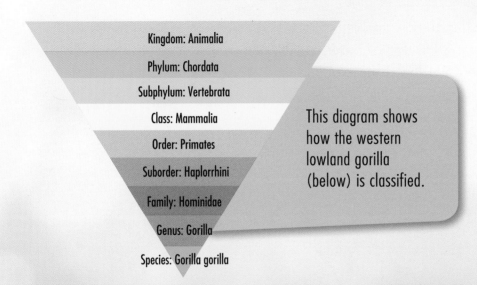

Kingdom: Animalia

Phylum: Chordata

Subphylum: Vertebrata

Class: Mammalia

Order: Primates

Suborder: Haplorrhini

Family: Hominidae

Genus: Gorilla

Species: Gorilla gorilla

This diagram shows how the western lowland gorilla (below) is classified.

Where Do Gorillas Live?

Gorillas live in **tropical** and **subtropical** forests in Africa. Some of the forests are in the mountains, and some cover areas of low, wet land. Gorillas live in these **habitats** because of the plants, trees, and rain.

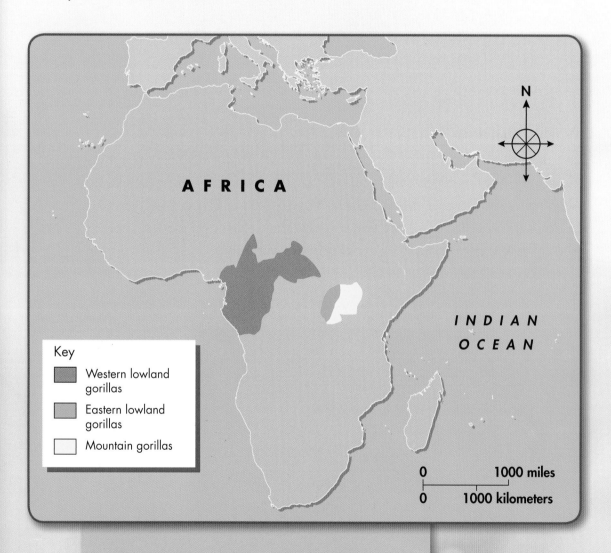

N

AFRICA

INDIAN OCEAN

Key

Western lowland gorillas

Eastern lowland gorillas

Mountain gorillas

0   1000 miles
0   1000 kilometers

This map shows where three of the four gorilla subspecies live. However, there are so few Cross River gorillas left that they cannot be shown here.

Forest habitats

Gorillas do well in tropical and subtropical forest habitats. A tropical forest is a forest of tall trees that grows where the temperature is warm all year. Subtropical forests also have tall trees, but they are a little farther from the equator and not quite as warm. Because of the higher **elevation** in their habitat, mountain gorillas experience cooler temperatures than other gorilla subspecies, especially at night.

The amount of rain determines the kinds of plants that grow in forest habitats. Some forests get a lot of rain—more than 100 inches (250 centimeters) a year. These forests are called **rain forests**. Gorillas that live in rain forests benefit from the many leafy plants that grow where water is plentiful.

Lowland gorillas

Some gorillas live in tropical forests that grow where the land is flat and low. The gorillas in these areas are called lowland gorillas. Lowland areas usually have a rainy season and a dry season. Plants in lowland areas include succulents (plants that can store water inside their cells) and thorny, short bushes. These plants provide lowland gorillas with food.

Lowland tropical forests sometimes have natural clearings where grasses and water plants grow. These are good food for lowland gorillas.

Mountain gorillas

Mountain gorillas live in the Virunga Mountain Range in Uganda, Rwanda, and the Democratic Republic of the Congo. During the rainy season, mountain gorillas live among tall trees with smooth bark and thick bushes. They eat the bark, leaves, stems, and fruits of these plants. During drier months, mountain gorillas move to areas where they can eat bamboo.

The many plants and trees in the tropical forest habitat provide gorillas with food, bedding, and spaces for play and rest.

DIAN FOSSEY

In 1966 Dian Fossey began studying mountain gorillas in eastern Africa. At first, the gorillas ran away whenever she tried to approach. Then she began to quietly copy the gorillas' behavior. She climbed trees and chomped on wild celery. Soon, Fossey could sit close to the gorillas without scaring them. She took photographs of the gorillas and studied their behavior for almost 20 years.

Dian Fossey worked hard to protect the mountain gorillas. She tried to stop hunters and people who wanted to make money by showing the gorillas to visitors. She also tried to keep cows from eating the grasses in the gorillas' habitat. Her work made poachers (illegal hunters) and farmers angry. Fossey was killed in Rwanda in 1985, probably by people who wanted to stop her work.

An organization that Dian Fossey started in 1978 still exists. It is called the Dian Fossey Gorilla Fund International, and it works to help protect gorillas.

Dian Fossey became the first human to experience a friendly touch by a mountain gorilla.

What Adaptations Help Gorillas Survive?

Over time, gorillas have developed characteristics that help them survive in the forests of Africa. These characteristics and behaviors are called **adaptations**. Mountain gorillas possess slightly different adaptations than lowland gorillas.

Arms and legs

A gorilla's long arms and short legs make it easy for it to walk on all fours. This way of walking spreads out the gorilla's heavy weight onto both its arms and legs. If a gorilla had to walk on just its legs, its bones, knees, and hips would soon wear down from the weight.

TUG-OF-WAR

Scientists estimate that a gorilla is over six times stronger than a human. A gorilla would win a game of tug-of-war even if six adult men were pulling on the other side!

Because gorillas are so large, they are not as fast or as flexible as other primates. They are not able to swing easily from tree branch to tree branch. Instead, gorillas use their long, strong arms to pull down branches, rip thick plants from the ground, and climb trees to find food.

Hands and feet

Gorillas have **opposable thumbs** and opposable big toes. This means that the thumb and big toe can face and touch the other fingers and toes. This allows gorillas to grasp small objects such as insects and vines with their hands and feet. The gorillas' grip also allows them to hold their babies carefully, peel stems, and build nests for sleeping.

Here you can see a gorilla's opposable big toe.

Look out for those teeth!

Gorillas have 32 teeth, many of which are huge molars. These molars allow gorillas to grind up tough plant parts so they can be swallowed. Gorillas also have teeth called canines. These pointy teeth are found on the sides of the mouth and help with ripping.

Male gorillas' canines are especially big. The males use these large, sharp teeth to defend females and their young from predators (animals that eat other animals) such as leopards.

Keeping warm

Gorillas must keep warm to survive. This is not a problem for lowland gorillas, as the temperatures where they live rarely drop below 68 °F (20 °C). However, some mountain gorillas live high up enough to experience near freezing temperatures at night.

Mountain gorillas have developed long, thick hair to keep them warm. In contrast, lowland gorillas have short hair. The hair on all gorillas protects them from insect bites.

Gorillas have also developed behaviors to keep themselves warm. On cold days, gorillas huddle close together for long periods of time. They use each other's body heat to stay warm.

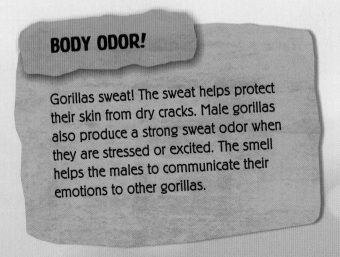

BODY ODOR!

Gorillas sweat! The sweat helps protect their skin from dry cracks. Male gorillas also produce a strong sweat odor when they are stressed or excited. The smell helps the males to communicate their emotions to other gorillas.

These mountain gorillas have long,
thick hair to keep them warm.

What Do Gorillas Eat?

Gorillas are herbivores, which means they mainly eat plants. Gorillas are not known to kill other animals for food, and few animals attack or feed on gorillas.

The types of plants gorillas eat depend on where they live. Mountain gorillas usually eat green plant parts such as leaves, vines, and stems. They also eat small amounts of fruit, roots, and tiny creatures such as worms and snails. Eastern lowland gorillas eat plants, and they also eat fruits when they can find them. Western lowland gorillas eat a lot of fruit as well as leaves, stems, and seeds.

Gorillas will travel outside their normal living area to find special food such as young bamboo stems.

A giant appetite

Gorillas spend about a third of their day eating. An adult male will eat up to 45 pounds (20 kilograms) of food each day. That is about the weight of a six-year-old child! Gorillas eat so much in order to get all the **nutrients** their large bodies need.

Gorillas are picky about their food. They will peel off the stem of a plant to eat the soft part inside. They leave behind the parts of the plants they do not like. Gorillas rarely drink water. Instead, the plants they eat contain the water they need. Gorillas also suck rainwater from their hair.

Top of the chain

A food chain is made up of a series of living things that are each dependent on the next as a source of food. Gorillas are usually at the top of their food chain.

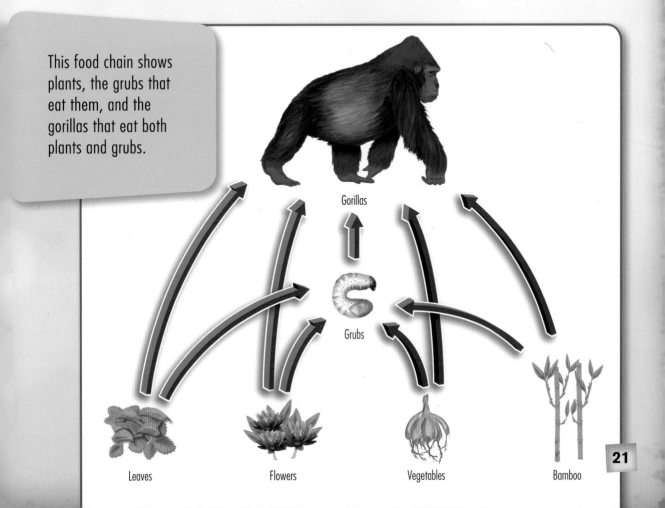

This food chain shows plants, the grubs that eat them, and the gorillas that eat both plants and grubs.

Gorillas

Grubs

Leaves

Flowers

Vegetables

Bamboo

What Is a Gorilla's Life Cycle?

Gorillas experience different stages of life, just as humans do. Gorillas are babies first, then children, and finally adults. When they are adults, gorillas can produce babies. The stages of growth from a creature's birth to its death are called its life cycle.

A baby is born

A baby gorilla grows inside its mother's body for about 8½ months. At birth, the baby gorilla weighs about 4½ pounds (2 kilograms). The baby starts drinking its mother's milk immediately. It depends on its mother for food, warmth, and protection.

Baby gorillas learn to climb onto their mothers' backs when they are six to seven months old. They hold on tight while their mother moves around.

Baby gorillas grow quickly. They begin to crawl at about nine weeks old. At about six to seven months old, baby gorillas can walk short distances. They start to eat plants, but they also keep drinking their mother's milk until they are about two years old.

Play is very important for young gorillas. They chase, wrestle, and join in games with each other. Baby gorillas also play with adults, jumping on them and giving them gentle bites.

Juvenile gorillas

Between the ages of three and six, young gorillas are known as juveniles. Juveniles practice skills such as peeling stems by copying the older gorillas. A juvenile gorilla still stays close to its mother, sharing her nest until she has her next baby three or four years later.

Juvenile gorillas like climbing trees. Since they are smaller and lighter than adults, they can climb more easily to find leaves high above the ground.

Teenage gorillas

Gorillas move into a stage called adolescence when they are about six years old. During this stage, they begin to turn into adults. They gain weight and grow larger. They become skilled at finding food. During adolescence, males grow taller and start to look different from females. The adolescent males are called "blackbacks" because, unlike the adult males, the hair on their backs is dark.

Here you can see adolescent males, a female, a baby, and an adult male. Can you tell which is which?

Adulthood

Gorillas reach adulthood when they are able to reproduce (have babies of their own). A female reaches adulthood at about eight years old. Most females have their first babies by the age of ten. Female gorillas usually have one baby at a time, every three to four years.

Male gorillas are fully grown and able to reproduce at about 11 or 12 years of age. At this time, silvery-gray hair grows across their backs and they become "silverbacks." Often, the new adult is chased away by the male leader of his group. The young silverback then starts a group of his own or takes over another silverback's group. As the leader of a group, the silverback will mate with the group's two or three female gorillas.

Gorillas live to about 35 years of age in the wild. In zoos, they can live up to the age of 50. Gorillas lose their teeth as they grow older. Without teeth, eating is difficult. An old gorilla becomes thin and weak.

This female gorilla is pregnant.

How Do Gorillas Behave?

Gorillas live together in family groups. The gorillas within a group eat, relax, and sleep close to each other.

Living in troops

A gorilla family group is called a troop. Each troop usually has 5 to 10 members, but some have up to 30. One strong male silverback leads the troop. Other members include one or two adolescent males, two or three females, and several juveniles and babies.

As the leader of the troop, the silverback makes all the decisions. The silverback decides where the troop will travel, when they will eat, and when they will rest. The silverback mates with each of the females in the troop. He is the father of all the young gorillas. Although gorillas are usually peaceful, a silverback will fight to protect his troop from predators such as crocodiles and humans.

Each troop is led by a silverback male.

Home range

The gorilla troop lives and travels in one general area. This area is called a home range. A troop's home range covers 1 to 6 square miles (2.5 to 16 square kilometers). Since many different kinds of plants grow in **tropical** forests, gorillas usually do not have to travel far to find food. Yet a troop always moves to a new eating space each day. This behavior saves forest plants from being destroyed.

Sometimes the home range of one troop overlaps with the home range of another. Gorillas usually do not fight over their area. Instead, the silverback leader simply moves his troop a safe distance away.

Troop members spread out when they eat, to avoid arguments over food.

How do new troops form?

Once a young silverback becomes an adult, he sets out to form his own troop. Sometimes he attracts females from other troops to join him. Or he might try to take over a troop from an older silverback by scaring him away. Silverbacks might even fight for the leadership of a troop. If the younger silverback loses, he will often spend time with other young adult males before he tries to win his own troop again.

Silverbacks try to scare their enemies away by showing their teeth, roaring, and beating their chests.

When a female gorilla becomes an adult, she leaves her family troop to join a new one. The female must respect the silverback in the new group. If the silverback does not earn her trust, the female may leave. Some females change troops two or three times before they settle down.

In a troop, a female's importance depends on how long she has known the silverback. Often, a female gorilla tries to join a silverback who is alone. That way, she automatically becomes the most important female in the troop.

Who grooms whom?

Gorillas groom each other based on their relationships. Grooming is when one animal cleans another animal's hair and skin. Younger females in a troop argue over who gets to groom the silverback. They want to win his approval. Usually, females do not groom each other, but every mother carefully grooms her young.

It is the mother's responsibility to groom these young gorillas. At the moment, they are busy playing!

A DAY IN THE LIFE OF A GORILLA

Gorillas spend most of their time eating and resting. They get up early in the morning when the sun rises. The troop moves to the spot where they will feed for the day. Then the gorillas eat all morning.

With full bellies, gorillas relax for four to six hours in the middle of the day. The babies and juveniles play with each other. The adults rest as they watch the young ones. Gorillas also use this rest time to cuddle. In the late afternoon, they set out to eat for a few more hours. Then they settle in for a long night's sleep when the sun goes down.

READY FOR BED

Gorillas make new sleeping nests every night. They gather leaves, twigs, and branches to tuck under and around themselves. Each gorilla makes its own nest, except for young ones under three years old. The babies sleep with their mothers.

LOOKING FOR MIZA

In 2007 a baby gorilla named Miza and her mother disappeared from their family group in Virunga National Park, in the Democratic Republic of the Congo. Miza's father, a silverback named Kabirizi, immediately moved his family group to a hiding spot high in the mountains. Then he searched for Miza and her mother. After several days, Kabirizi found Miza in the forest. Sadly, Miza's mother was never found. Miza's story has been recorded in a book called *Looking for Miza*.

This western lowland gorilla
is eating a meal of leaves.

How Intelligent Are Gorillas?

Gorillas have large heads that contain large brains. These big, complex brains make them capable of learning, remembering, using tools, and communicating with each other. Gorillas are curious animals.

Young gorillas learn skills by copying older gorillas and then practicing. For example, baby gorillas try to make their own sleeping nests from the time they are 18 months old. At first, the young gorillas only pull a few grass stems over themselves. With practice over the next two years, they learn how to make neat, comfortable nests.

Baby gorillas learn new skills by copying the behavior of older gorillas.

Using tools

In 2005 scientists observed gorillas using tools for the first time. A female gorilla in the Democratic Republic of the Congo used a stick to test the depth of water before wading into a river. A second gorilla used a tree stump as a bridge. Since 2005 scientists have observed other wild gorillas using rocks to smash open palm nuts. In Cameroon, Cross River gorillas have used sticks, rocks, and lumps of dirt to chase away humans.

SET FREE

Damian Aspinall raised a baby gorilla named Kwibi at his **conservation** organization in Kent, England. When Kwibi was five years old, Aspinall released him into a **rain forest** in West Africa. Five years later, in 2010, Aspinall returned to the spot of Kwibi's release. He called for Kwibi using sounds from the gorilla's childhood. Amazingly, Kwibi recognized the sounds and Aspinall. Kwibi immediately sat down next to Aspinall. Then he playfully climbed on Aspinall's back.

Damian Aspinall is reunited with Kwibi as several members of Kwibi's troop look on.

Gorilla communication

Gorillas make 22 different sounds to express love, joy, fear, sadness, anger, pride, and other emotions. When gorillas are happy, they make purring sounds. When they are upset, they cough or bark. A low rumbling sound can be heard when gorillas are laughing. Gorillas even cry, using soft sounds rather than tears. Baby gorillas whimper or scream if they are scared or left alone.

Gorillas also communicate emotions with the expressions on their faces. With a stern look, the lead silverback can stop his females from arguing. When angry, gorillas press their lips firmly together and stare straight ahead. When afraid, gorillas open their mouths wide, show their teeth, and shift their eyes back and forth. Young gorillas smile when they are play-fighting.

Gorillas use body movements to communicate. This male is beating his chest to scare off an enemy. The "pok-pok" noise of the chest beating can be heard over 650 feet (200 meters) away!

FRANCINE "PENNY" PATTERSON

Francine "Penny" Patterson has studied communication between gorillas and humans for almost 40 years. In 1972 she began working with a one-year-old gorilla named Koko. Over time, Patterson taught Koko over 1,000 words in sign language. Patterson says that Koko also understands about 2,000 English words. Koko responds with sign language or obedience to a command.

Patterson established the Gorilla Foundation with other scientists. This organization works to protect wild gorillas and study gorilla intelligence.

Penny Patterson (left) is asking Koko if she is hungry, and Koko is replying that she is!

What Threats Do Gorillas Face?

Gorillas are **endangered** animals. They may become **extinct** because of hunting, loss of their **habitat**, and disease. Humans are the greatest threat to gorillas.

Hunting gorillas

Gorillas are often hunted for their meat. Many people in Africa are poor and need food. They cannot afford to buy expensive meats such as pork or chicken. So they buy the meat of wild animals such as gorillas and elephants. Meat from wild animals is called bushmeat. Hunters make money by selling bushmeat to restaurants and local people. Hunters often break the law by killing gorillas on protected land.

Some people hunt gorillas as a sport. They want to collect parts of gorillas to show off to others. Sadly, a gorilla's hands or head may be turned into a trophy. Sometimes, hunters set traps for other animals, but gorillas accidentally get caught in them.

If a gorilla gets caught in a trap like this, it can be seriously injured or even die.

Habitat loss

As human populations grow, people look for new places to live and work. Sometimes people cut down the trees in African forests to make space for farms and houses. People also use the trees for firewood.

Companies clear trees off the land to make money. Mining companies want to dig for a metal called coltan. Coltan is used to make cell phones. Other companies chop down the trees so that the wood can be used to build houses.

Companies cut down forest trees to sell the wood as a building material.

Problems for gorillas

As people cut down the forests, gorillas must move to new places or live in open areas. Mountain gorillas have begun to live higher up in the mountains, but the cold, wet temperatures at these heights can cause illness. Cleared land makes food hard to find for lowland gorillas.

With the trees and bushes gone, some gorillas search for food in farmers' fields. Often, people attack the gorillas to scare them away. The silverback leader will try to defend his troop. He may be killed, and the troop will scatter. The gorillas are unlikely to survive without their leader.

EASY PICKINGS

Cleared land makes hunting gorillas easier. **Tropical** forests are often too thick with trees for humans to move quickly. With cleared land, hunters can use vehicles to get close to the gorillas.

Diseases

Safari vacations, which allow tourists to see gorillas up close, are popular in Africa. Money paid by the visitors helps the local people. However, people can spread diseases to gorillas if they get too close. Gorillas do not have any protection from many human diseases. A disease such as measles can be deadly.

Why should humans care about gorillas?

Gorillas are quiet, peaceful animals that present no danger to humans unless they are threatened. They help keep the forest habitat healthy. Gorillas eat and distribute seeds, so new plants will grow. If gorillas become extinct, the chance to know more about these "gentle giants" would be lost forever.

It can be thrilling to see gorillas up close in the wild. However, if the gorillas become too comfortable around humans, they may be less likely to run away from hunters.

How Can People Help Gorillas?

Humans are the main reason that gorillas are **endangered**. However, humans are also working hard to save gorillas and **conserve** their **habitats**.

Conservation organizations

Conservation organizations raise money to rescue and nurse injured gorillas. They also help enforce laws against poaching and help poor people find food sources other than bushmeat. Some conservation groups work to protect gorilla habitats from being destroyed.

What can you do?

- You can join conservation groups, such as the World Wildlife Fund (WWF) and Conservation International, and perhaps donate some pocket money every now and then.

- Encourage your family not to buy furniture made from the wood of **rain forest** trees.

- If you go shopping for food with your parents, you can ask them to buy goods that have been produced in an environmentally friendly way. Food labels will give information on this. Fair Trade Certified goods ensure that money is earned by local people, which may mean they do not have to take part in activities that may harm gorillas.

- Read about gorillas and tell your friends and family about what you find out. The more people who know about endangered gorillas, the better.

- Finally, make sure you recycle as much as possible. This means that materials such as wood can be saved and reused. That way, more trees do not need to be cut down.

Scientists believe there may be only about 200 Cross River gorillas left. The Cross River gorilla is the most endangered of all gorilla subspecies.

What Does the Future Hold for Gorillas?

The future of gorillas is not certain. These gentle giants will become **extinct** if their **habitats** disappear and if they continue to be hunted in large numbers.

However, there is hope for gorillas. **Conservation** organizations have helped to keep the numbers of living gorillas more constant. African governments are working to maintain peace, so that people will travel to see the gorillas. With vacations called "eco-tours," local people earn money by leading groups through the forest in ways that are safe for the animals and the visitors. Individuals and groups around the world are working hard to save the gorillas and their forest habitats.

WALKING TALL

The Aspinall Foundation rescues sick or injured gorillas. One of the foundation's rescued gorillas, Ambam, has become famous. In 2010 an animal researcher filmed the 21-year-old silverback strolling around on just his feet. The researcher posted the video on YouTube. Thousands of people have now watched Ambam walk around like a human. Scientists believe Ambam walks upright rather than on all fours so that he can carry food with his hands and see over the wall at feeding time.

If people work hard to protect gorillas and their habitats, there is a good chance they will survive.

Gorilla Profile

sagittal crest

large forehead

wide, flat nose

small eyes

black to brown-gray hair

long, strong arms

Species: Western gorilla

Weight: Adult males weigh 300 to 500 pounds (135 to 220 kilograms); adult females weigh 150 to 200 pounds (70 to 90 kilograms)

Height: Adult males are 5 feet, 7 inches to 6 feet (1.7 to 1.8 meters) tall; adult females are up to 5 feet (1.5 meters) tall

Habitat: Tropical mountain and lowland forests

Diet: Fruit, leaves, stems, flowers, seeds, bark, roots, and some insects

Number of young: A single infant is born after 8½ months of pregnancy. Females will give birth about every 4 years after they have reached maturity at about 8 years of age.

Birth weight: 4 to 5 pounds (1.8 to 2.3 kilograms)

Life expectancy: About 35 years in the wild, and up to 50 years in captivity

Glossary

adaptation body part or behavior of a living thing that helps it survive in a particular habitat

classify group living things together by their similarities and differences

conservation protection or restoration of wildlife and the natural environment

conserve protect from harm or destruction

elevation height of the land above sea level

endangered living thing that is at risk of dying out

evolve change gradually over time

extinct living thing that has died out

habitat natural environment of a living thing

mammal animal that has fur or hair, gives birth to live young, and feeds its young on milk from the mother

nutrient substance that provides a living thing with the nourishment it needs to grow and live

opposable thumb thumb that can face and touch the fingers on the same hand

rain forest forest with tall, thickly growing trees in an area with high rainfall

species group of similar living things that can mate with each other

subtropical regions of Earth that border the tropics

tropical regions of Earth around the equator

Find Out More

Books

Hatkoff, Juliana, et al. *Looking for Miza: The True Story of the Mountain Gorilla Family Who Rescued One of Their Own*. New York: Scholastic, 2008.

Moore, Heidi. *Great Naturalists: Dian Fossey*. Chicago: Raintree, 2009.

Solway, Andrew. *Classifying Living Things: Classifying Mammals*. Chicago: Heinemann Library, 2009.

Websites

www.gorillafund.org
Find out lots of information about gorillas and how people can help protect them on the website of the Dian Fossey Gorilla Fund International.

http://kids.nationalgeographic.com/kids/animals/creaturefeature/mountain-gorilla/
Learn all about mountain gorillas at this website, which includes videos.

Organizations to contact

World Wildlife Fund
www.wwf.org
WWF works to protect animals and nature.

Endangered Species International
www.endangeredspeciesinternational.org/index.php
This organization focuses on saving endangered animals around the world.

The Gorilla Foundation
www.koko.org
This organization aims to help save gorillas from extinction. It is especially known for its work with Koko the gorilla.

Index

adaptations 16–17
adolescents 24, 26
apes 6

babies 8, 17, 22–23,
    25, 26, 30, 32,
    34, 45
behavior 26–31, 32–35
blackbacks 24
bonobos 6
bushmeat 36, 40

captivity 25, 45
chest-beating 28, 34
chimpanzees 6, 8
classification 10–11
communication 18,
    34–35
conservation 15,
    40–41, 42
Cross River gorillas 11,
    12, 41

diseases 38

eco-tourism 42
endangered animals 5,
    36, 40, 41
extinction 36, 39, 42

facial expressions 34
female gorillas 7, 25, 26,
    28, 29, 45
food 13, 14, 20–21,
    27, 31
food chains 21
forest habitats 12–13,
    14, 37
Fossey, Dian 15

gibbons 6
grooming 29

habitat loss 37
habitats 12–14
hair 8
hands 4–5
height 7
herbivores 20
home range 27
humans 4, 6, 36
hunting 36, 38, 42

intelligence 5, 32–35

juveniles 23, 26, 30

knuckle-walking 8

lemurs 4
life cycle 22–25
life expectancy 25, 45
logging 37
lowland gorillas 11, 13,
    16, 18, 20, 38

male gorillas 7, 8, 18,
    21, 24, 25, 26, 27,
    28, 29
mammals 4
mating 26
monkeys 4
mountain gorillas 11, 13,
    14, 15, 16, 18, 19,
    20, 38
movement 7, 8, 16,
    23, 42

nests 17, 23, 30, 32

opposable thumbs and
    toes 17
orangutans 4, 6

Patterson, Francine 35
physical characteristics
    4–5, 6–9, 17–18,
    44, 45
play 23, 29, 30, 34
poaching 15, 36, 40, 42
predators 18, 26
primates 4–5, 6
profile 44–45

rain forests 13

sign language 35
silverbacks 8, 25, 26,
    27, 28, 29, 38
smell, sense of 9
species and subspecies
    11
stomachs 7
strength 16

teeth 18, 25, 28
threats 36–39
tool use 33
troops 18, 25,
    26–29, 38

vision 4, 9

walking 7, 8, 16, 34, 42
weight 7